MW01047312

2013

U.S. Special Forces

BY LINDA BOZZO

amicus
high interest

Amicus High Interest is an imprint of Amicus
P.O. Box 1329, Mankato, MN 56002
www.amicuspublishing.us

Library of Congress Cataloging-in-Publication Data
Bozzo, Linda.
 U.S. Special Forces / by Linda Bozzo.
    pages cm. -- (Serving in the military)
 Includes index.
 Summary: "An introduction to what the US Special Forces
are, including the Green Berets, Navy SEALs, and Marine
Force Recon, what recruits do, and jobs soldiers could learn.
Includes descriptions of missions to find Osama bin Laden and
to rescue an American aid worker in Somalia"--Provided by
publisher.
 Audience: Grades K-3.
 ISBN 978-1-60753-394-8 (library binding) -- ISBN 978-1-
60753-442-6 (ebook)
 1. Special forces (Military science)--United States--Juvenile
literature. I. Title.
 UA34.S64B658 2014
 356'.16--dc23
                                    2013001413

Editor   Wendy Dieker
Series Designer   Kathleen Petelinsek
Page production   Red Line Editorial, Inc.

Photo Credits
Naval Special Warfare, cover; Amy Sancetta/AP Images,
4; Mass Communication Specialist 2nd Class Meranda
Keller/U.S. Navy, 7; Cpl. Andrew S. Avitt/U.S. Marine Corps,
8; Spc. Melissa C. Parrish, 49th Public Affairs Detachment,
Airborne/U.S. Army, 10; Sgt. Grant Mathes/U.S. Army, 13;
Spc. Anna K. Perry/U.S. Army, 14; Mass Communication
Specialist 3rd Class Adam Henderson/U.S. Navy, 17; Sgt.
Derek Kuhn/U.S. Army, 18; Lt. Cmdr. Cheol Kang/U.S. Navy,
21; U.S. Marine Corps, 22, 25, 26; Lt. Iain Jones/U.S. Navy,
29

Printed in the United States at Corporate Graphics in North
Manakato, Minnesota
5-2013 / 1150
10 9 8 7 6 5 4 3 2 1

Table of Contents

Enemies crashed planes into these buildings in New York City.

Special Forces on a Mission

It was September 11, 2001. America was attacked. Men flew planes into buildings. Thousands of people were killed. It was a sad day. People were angry. A man named Osama bin Laden planned these attacks. He was wanted for this crime. The best U.S. **special forces** soldiers started looking for him. It took almost ten years, but they found where he was hiding.

U.S. spies found bin Laden in Pakistan. It was night on May 2, 2011. U.S. Navy SEALs rode in two choppers. They flew in low. The enemy radar didn't see them. The SEALs dropped from the helicopters. They shot their way into a house. They found bin Laden in an upstairs room. The SEALs shot and killed him. They took his computers. They got information to help stop more attacks on America. Success!

 Why couldn't the radar see the SEALs?

SEALs practice a helicopter mission at dusk. They must be ready.

A The helicopters flew in low under the radar. They also had special parts that kept the choppers quiet.

Marines must be ready to defend against enemies.

 Are there other special forces?

Each branch of the armed services has special forces. These teams of soldiers get special training. They are tough. They do the most important missions. The Navy SEALs train for **combat** missions. The Army Green Berets train to sneak up on enemies. Marine Force Recon trains to be spies. These teams all have special jobs.

 Yes! Each branch of the armed services has several special units. There are even joint groups that do not belong to any one branch.

Green Berets train in an obstacle course called "Nasty Nick."

How did the Green Berets get their name?

Green Berets

One armed service unit is the Army Special Forces. But they are best known as the Green Berets. These men go on some of the hardest missions. They work in the worst weather. They are highly skilled in combat. Green Berets can move quickly to any part of the world. Their missions are often secret.

 The Green Berets are named after the type of hat they wear. It's a green beret, of course.

Green Berets get special training. They go to the **Airborne School** to learn how to jump out of planes. They learn to survive if they are lost in the wilderness. They learn to find their way on land in the dark. These soldiers train to surprise the enemy. They must strike fast. Missions are quick and dangerous.

Green Berets learn how to jump out of planes high in the air.

These Afghan soldiers trained with Green Berets to learn special skills.

The Green Berets hunt for enemies. They look for people who attack our country. Green Berets sneak behind enemy lines to spy. They **raid** enemy camps to take their **weapons**. They work on other kinds of missions too. Green Berets might work in friendly countries. They teach soldiers how to fight.

Navy SEALs

The SEALs are part of the navy, so many missions are in or around water. But some missions take place in the air or on land. SEALs are some of the best soldiers. They often work in secret. Only men can be SEALs. This is because the jobs they could have can be very dangerous!

 What does SEAL stand for?

Navy SEALs learn how to climb onto rigs in the ocean.

SEAL stands for Sea, Air, and Land. These are the places where the sailors work.

Training to be a Navy SEAL lasts 25 weeks. Some say it is the hardest military training. Sailors run and swim long distances. They learn to use scuba gear to work underwater. Rescue skills are taught. SEALs practice jumping from planes using a **parachute**. They also learn to take apart bombs. Many sailors never finish the training. Only the best become SEALs.

SEALs are brave. They jump out of planes.

Navy SEALs take on missions all over the world. These missions are usually secret. SEALs spy on enemies. They lead beach strikes. Raids are carried out. They capture enemies. Sometimes they have to kill enemies. SEALs also do rescue missions. They find missing soldiers. They do important work.

SEALs are on a mission near Korea.

Marine special forces are trained to spy. They are called Force Recon.

Marine Force Recon

The U.S. Marine Corps has a few special units. Force Recon is one of them. Recon is short for **reconnaissance**. This means they are spies. Their jobs take place deep behind enemy lines. They learn about the enemy. But they can't get caught. There are times when they have to fight. But their main job is spying.

Marines in Force Recon need skills that will help them find and watch the enemy. They train on land. They even train on skis in the snow. But they train most in the water. They learn how to work with scuba gear. More advanced training includes special parachuting skills. These marines know how to gather information in all kinds of places.

 What kind of parachuting do Force Recon marines learn?

Marines measure how deep the water is and make a map.

A   Marines are taught HALO. This stands for High Altitude, Low Opening. This type of jump makes it harder to be seen as they drop.

Marines jump out of a chopper into the water.

On the job, marines in Force Recon watch. They listen. They learn what the enemy is doing. They see who has weapons. They find out where enemy soldiers are. Force Recon tells their findings to the combat marines. This information helps them plan missions.

Serving Our Country

When there are dangerous missions, U.S. special forces are up to the job. They train hard. They are the best soldiers. The spies get facts about the enemies. Some soldiers hunt for enemies. Others rescue people trapped behind enemy lines. In 2011, aid workers were kidnapped in Somalia. SEALs to the rescue! The team found the workers. They saved the day!

Special forces soldiers are ready for dangerous missions!

29

Glossary

Airborne School A school at Fort Benning, Georgia, where soldiers go to learn how to jump out of planes.

combat Fighting in a war.

parachute A large piece of strong and light fabric used to make a safe landing when jumping from a plane.

raids Sudden attacks.

reconnaissance Spying; watching enemies to get information.

special forces Teams of elite soldiers who receive more training to perform special missions.

weapons Something used to fight, such as guns or bombs.

Read More

David, Jack. *Army Green Berets*. Minneapolis, MN. Bellwether Media, 2009.

Lunis, Natalie. *The Takedown of Osama bin Laden*. New York, NY. Bearport Publishing, 2012.

Nelson, Drew. *Navy SEALs*. *New York, NY*. Gareth Stevens Publishing, 2012.

Sandler, Michael. *Marine Force Recon in Action*. New York, NY. Bearport Publishing, 2008.

Websites

Official Website of the Navy SEALs
http://www.sealswcc.com/seal-default.aspx

Special Forces: GoArmy.com
http://www.goarmy.com/special-forces.html

U.S. Marine Corps Forces Special Operations Command
http://www.marsoc.marines.mil/

Index

About the Author

Linda Bozzo is the author of more than 30 books for the school and library market. Visit her website at www. lindabozzo.com. She would like to thank all of the men and women in the military for their outstanding service to our country.